THE EVERYDAY COMMISSION

THE Everyday COMMISSION

SONLIFE

Harold Shaw Publishers
Wheaton, Illinois

Library of Congress Cataloging-in-Publication Data

Spader, Dann.
    The everyday commission : discover the joy of partnership with God /
    Dann Spader and Gary Mayes
        p.   cm.
    ISBN 0-87788-239-8
    1. Great Commission (Bible) 2. Christian Life —1960-   I. Mayes,
Gary. II. Title.
BV2074.S63 1994
266--dc20   94-3947
                                                             CIP

99 98 97 96 95 94

10 9 8 7 6 5 4 3 2 1

CONTENTS

... and on the 7th day thou shalt clear the platform, check the sound system, replace the broken guitar string, change the microphone battery, select the chorus transparencies, prepare the chord sheets, replace the broken overhead projector lens, tune the piano, attach the new drum heads, lead 2 worship services ....and rest.

A Crisis of Purpose

Crisp mountain air stung their faces as the glass doors shut behind them. "We're outta here," laughed Ron, holding the door open for Alan. "They won't miss us for hours."

Their afternoon trek through the quaint resort town had no agenda, no deadline, no nagging to-do list. It was the kind of leisurely paced Saturday stroll that invites reflection and inspires deeply personal conversation.

The enticing aroma of freshly ground coffee escaped through the doorway of a storefront café. With barely a knowing glance, Ron and Alan turned inside and settled into a corner table. Around the time of their second refill, talk of sports, kids, and the lake outside shifted to secret concerns and long-suppressed fears.

"I'm so glad the girls wanted to linger without us in that art store for a while," began Alan. "There are some nagging questions I've wanted to talk about for some time, and I could use your help in trying to sort them out. This weekend getaway came at a time when I really needed it."

"It comes at the right time for me too," Ron answered. "This past Christmas season wore me out. Our church calendar was filled more than usual, and family commitments seemed endless."

"It's more than holiday craziness and fatigue," said Alan. "I've been looking closely at my life, and I'm afraid something's missing. Something doesn't feel right inside."

"What are you talking about?" Ron interrupted. "I've known you for seven years, and you are one family with your act together. You guys have your priorities in order. Your kids are great. Your business is booming. Your new venture into graphic design is exploding."

"I know. The way God has blessed my family and my business makes me feel guilty for struggling with these things at all."

"Why don't you start at the beginning? The girls don't expect to meet us for hours, so there's no rush."

Alan fiddled with his placemat, unconsciously tearing little pieces off with his fork, and groped for a place to begin. "I'm not sure I can put my finger on it, but somehow I feel like the investments of my time and energy—*my life*—don't add up to much.

"Maybe I am struggling with the hardest question of all," he continued. "What is the purpose of my life? I know my business is not *the* purpose. Sure, it's a stewardship of abilities and opportunities God has given me, but what do I do that has eternal value? I'm glad we're close friends, but sometimes I get really jealous of you. I mean, God called you to be a pastor, and he only called me to be a printer. Everything you do makes a difference in the lives of other people. Everything I print winds up in someone's trash can—sooner or later. What you do has eternal value and significance. Sometimes the things I do around the church feel so insignificant to me, like I'm just a cog in the wheel.

"I've been fighting through these questions for months now. I'm sure it's not a mid-life crisis thing. I just have this burning desire to be used by God, and I don't know how to satisfy it. Does any of this make sense?"

Alan stared out the window for what felt like a long time and then added, "You're my best friend, but maybe you can't relate. I've never shared this with anyone."

Ron swirled the final drops of coffee around in the bottom of his cup, struggling for a way to respond. "This may be hard to understand, but the truth is, I feel the same way."

"What?" Alan betrayed his surprise.

"I know you don't expect to hear that from your pastor, but it's true. Every week I do the same things. I study for and then deliver a message or two, always wishing they had been a little better. I meet with a few people who are ready to talk through difficult issues in their lives, and I worry about those who need to talk but aren't willing to open up. I write letters, meet with committees, conduct staff meetings, contact visitors, solve problems. . . . It often feels as if I'm only the grease that keeps the wheels turning. I wonder if we really are making the progress we claim. And in my heart I sense that something is missing. I have a craving to be used by God in mighty ways, and I fear it will never happen."

"Wait a minute," Alan interrupted. "Only last summer you were honored as alumnus of the year by your alma mater. Your peers respect you, the church is doing well, and your kids are some of the greatest teenagers I have ever known. I don't get it."

"I'm afraid that maybe the fire once burning inside is gone. When I was in seminary, we would plot and dream about reclaiming whole communities for Christ. We talked about lives being changed, about people coming to Christ, about people reaching their peers, and about revival in the land. I had such a sense of urgency, conviction, and passion. I didn't really have a plan or strategy, but it didn't matter. Now I have plans, goals, budgets, and ministry experience, but I'm low on fire. I even wonder if the plans and programs of our church are accomplishing what they should be. . . . Sorry. You started telling me about your feelings, and I took over with my own. I guess I needed to open up, too."

"There's nothing to be sorry about. As a matter of fact, you've just helped me understand what's going on inside of me. You mentioned a longing to be powerfully used by God. That's it! The more Jesus becomes the center of my life, the more I want to serve him in substantial ways. I figured I needed to do more at the church, but just doing more isn't the answer."

"It doesn't make you uncomfortable to hear that your pastor has struggles like these?" Ron asked.

"Are you kidding? It encourages me. Being friends doesn't keep me from putting you on that 'pastor pedestal' from time to time. In fact, knowing things don't come easily for you motivates me to keep hacking away, too. I think you should share this with the board. Maybe even the whole church. Let others see the smoldering embers in your life. Let them help you fan them into a roaring blaze again."

Ron hesitated, wondering how his board might react. "I don't know. I'm not sure I'm ready to spill it all out yet."

THE BOARD

Ron had often talked about honesty and openness with his board, yet rarely were his own comments as vulnerable and raw as those he was about to make. He looked around the makeshift conference table in the church library and wondered if the people seated there would be able to help or even understand. After a silent prayer he began.

"During my portion of the board meeting I usually focus on ministry direction, biblical principles, leadership skills, or team development. However, today I want to share some personal issues. I would like to ask for your prayers and your input.

"Three weeks ago, when Sue and I were away in the mountains with Alan and his wife, Al and I began to talk about direction and purpose in our lives. I told him of some concerns I have—concerns and fears that are not easily put into words. He urged me to share my thoughts with all of you. Although I was hesitant at first, I realized it would be good to talk these things through with you.

"For some time now I have been wrestling with a deep sense that I am missing something. Something isn't quite right. I'm afraid I am not making the kind of impact with my life that I feel called to. I love this church and am proud of what has happened here, but I worry that we as a church aren't making the kind of impact we could or should be making. I fear that perhaps I have—and maybe all of us have—become satisfied with the status quo. I long for us to be used by God in powerful ways, and I fear it isn't happening and maybe never will."

No one moved, yet no one looked directly at Ron or at anyone else. Some board members feared their pastor was preparing to announce his resignation. Others thought he had been working too hard and needed a break. Most felt he needed encouragement. For a moment that seemed to last hours, questions, fears, and more than a little confusion raced through the minds of every person around that table. Then, almost spontaneously, all spoke at once trying to help him feel better.

"Pastor, you have been used by God to guide this church for eight years."

"That's right! When you came we averaged 125 people on a Sunday, and now our attendance regularly breaks the 600 mark."

"We have a full-time staff of four pastors, a thriving preschool, a new building, and solid finances."

"Thanks, but I'm not fishing for compliments," said Ron, breaking in. "I know we have grown, and that great things are going on here. But very little of our growth has come from evangelism. Lately very little of my time goes toward building relationships with or reaching out to non-Christians. I have no non-Christian friends anymore. Almost all of our ministries are geared toward nurturing believers. I fear we haven't helped them reach beyond their comfort zone to touch the lives of people without Christ. Our youth pastor puts me to shame with his aggressive balance of nurture *and evangelism*."

Before anyone could speak up, Ron added, "Please don't hear my ramblings as an accusation. As the shepherd of this body and one who really wants to make a difference, I am just struggling to figure out why I feel so uneasy and what steps should be taken to correct things. You are my partners in leadership here, so I need your help."

Finally able to verbalize his primary concern, one board member interrupted, thumping his pencil for emphasis. "Ron, are you telling us in some roundabout way that you want to resign?"

"No, Tom, I am not announcing anything. I feel as strongly now as ever that this is where God wants me. I also believe the uneasiness in my spirit is part of God's work to renew and retool my life. I just wanted to involve you in that process of change. I need you and your input."

Joan, a former missionary and now head of the church's missions committee, had said little to this point. Clearing her throat, she spoke up. "Ron, I've been listening, and I want you to know I admire your zeal and commitment to serving Christ and serving us. We are all committed to you as a person and as our pastor. But as I have listened, one thought kept occurring to me. We are a healthy church precisely because we nurture believers and help them grow in their faith. God has blessed us and allowed us to see people come to Christ. And we have been faithful in supporting missionaries who are carrying out the great commission around the world. It seems to me that we are doing what we should."

"Joan, I love your heart and respect your wisdom," replied Ron, "but I think that is exactly my point. The great commission is not just a clarion call to missions; it is our *local* mandate as well. We aren't called to do one thing here while we send missionaries to do 'the great commission' somewhere else. We all serve under the same mandate. And I've realized something else: Jesus never used the term *the great commission*. He wanted us to touch people around us, and all over the world. But it's easy to think that we can't do it, that only certain people are called to 'do' the great commission. But Jesus meant it more as an everyday commission, for everyday people like you and like me."

Growing concerned that this discussion wasn't leading to a conclusion and aware that it was his responsibility to guard against lengthy, meandering meetings, the board chairman broke in. He suggested these matters needed time for simmering. He also suggested that in the meantime they might all pray for Ron, the church, and the lessons God wanted them to learn.

After a closing prayer, the meeting was adjourned. Everyone agreed that Ron should continue to search the Scriptures, search his heart, and allow God to direct his convictions. It was the beginning of a hope that the Holy Spirit would use Ron's restless spirit to challenge the entire church. They promised to resume this discussion in next month's meeting.

THE MISSIONARY

A few days later, Joan stopped by the church to speak with Ron, who stood and welcomed her into his study.

"I can't stop thinking about your comments at our meeting. You touched a nerve that made me more restless than I have felt in a long time."

Ron chuckled. "It seems a little restlessness is going around."

"Well, at our meeting you said something about the great commission being a local church responsibility, or something like that," Joan said. "At first it made me mad. I felt that all of a sudden you were shortchanging missions. But the more I thought about it, the more I recognized you couldn't be more right. Even missionaries, once they leave home, settle into one local area in which to carry out the great commission. The real work is always done one local area at a time in the midst of relationships between people. It makes no difference what country or culture you are called to because it is the same work."

"Exactly! You just gave me the words I needed!" interrupted Ron. "I know that my questions are answered in Jesus' mandate for us. I'm not sure what all the questions are, let alone what the answers will be, but the more I have acknowledged and discussed the growing burden in my heart, the more I find the embers of my passion coming to life."

"Ron, you need to let the whole church body become partners with you in this reawakening," urged Joan. "Every one of us on the board has been deeply absorbed by these same thoughts since you shared them with us. Your honesty and your passion to serve Christ have moved us to prayer and personal reflection in new ways. Why not let everyone join in?"

THE SERMON

Ron stepped to the pulpit while the last strains of the organ faded. As he opened his Bible and laid out his notes, the members of his congregation settled into their seats. Their attentive expressions and warm glances were indicators of the teachable spirit characterizing the people of this church.

"Today's message is going to be a bit different. You might say it's not a sermon at all. Rather, it is an invitation.

"Awhile ago the Spirit of God launched me on a journey, and today I want to invite all of you to join me in it." Ron stepped out from behind the pulpit and began to open his heart.

"For some time now, there has been a seed of discontent germinating inside me. It's not a matter of morality or something I've even known how to describe until recently. A month ago, Sue and I spent the weekend in the mountains with Alan and Judy Erickson, two of our good friends. God used that weekend getaway and Alan's listening ears to help me begin sorting out my feelings.

"At the heart of it all has been what I would call a 'crisis of purpose.' I was wrestling with the patterns and priorities of my life and the life of this church. I looked back to the days when I first felt God calling me to serve in ministry. Those were days of bold dreams about 'conquering the world' for Jesus. They were naive in some ways, but filled with a desire to make an indelible mark for Christ.

"I look back over the past eight years here, and I see wonderful growth and joy shared by the people of this body. But I also look at the community around us and wonder if we really are making the impact God has called us to make. I look at the patterns of my life, and I wonder if my lack of involvement with nonbelievers fits with God's eternal priorities.

"As I have rambled about these thoughts with a few friends and with the board here at the church, some have worried that I am overworked, discouraged, or getting itchy for a change. I assure you, I am not having a mid-life crisis. I am OK. I do work a little too hard at times; who doesn't? And, true, I am a little restless. Yet I am encouraged by the way God is working and has worked in our church. I am more committed than ever to this body and to the work God has for us. I believe that this restlessness, this ache of my spirit, is a work of God to sharpen me as a person and as a pastor.

"I have found that in some form, everyone I have spoken with shares the same hunger to make more of an impact for Christ. Every true Christian has a deeply felt, genuine desire to be used by God in significant ways. I believe that each of you senses this same hunger.

"So today I want to invite you to become my partners on a journey. A journey that might cause discomfort as well as elation. A journey that might shake up some of our patterns as a church and give birth to new priorities. A journey to rekindle our passion for carrying on the work of Christ in this generation. A journey where we allow God to refocus our attention. A journey that I must take if I am to remain faithful to the work God has already begun in my life.

"I don't know all of the answers. But I do know that they are there to be found in the life of Christ. And I think I am beginning to understand what questions we must ask. I ask you to join me in asking these simple questions:

Q: What should our driving passion and purpose be as followers of Christ and as his church?

Q: How does that purpose make a difference in the patterns and priorities of my life?

Q: What are the implications of these priorities for the way we do things as a church?

Q: How would this purpose affect our involvement in national and international efforts?

"Next Sunday we will begin this journey by taking a close look at the great commission. I will be studying this passage all week as if looking at it for the first time. We'll learn together what God wants to say to us."

FOR YOU, THE READER

Ron, Alan, Joan, and the rest of the people of this church are composites. They represent pastors, elders, church leaders, and believers like you and me. They represent people who refuse to find contentment in oiling the machinery of the church, people who will not settle for the mere appearance of church health.

These are people who have discovered a burning desire to be used by God in powerful ways. They are people like you! You wouldn't be reading this book if you weren't hungry for your church and your own life to be effective in carrying out the work of Christ.

Our format is simple because we believe that the mandate of Christ is simple. We will merely ask the questions Ron challenged the people of his church to consider. It is our prayer that this book might provide you with the substance needed to refuel and retool your life and the life of your church.

To help you personalize this material, each chapter will end with a series of questions for reflection. If you are studying this book as part of a group, these questions could serve as good discussion starters. Whatever your approach, don't rush. Use a pen or pencil to record your thoughts, and enjoy the opportunity these questions create for the Spirit of God to direct you in a personal way.

QUESTIONS FOR REFLECTION

1. On a scale of 1 to 10, how would you rate the health of your church right now? What are some of the things that make you enthused and some of the dynamics that cause you to be concerned?

2. If God is going to do anything through your life, what would you like him to do? What would you like to leave as the legacy of your life? Try to put words to the longing you have felt.

3. Try to estimate what percentage of people in your church feel a deep longing to be significantly used by God, as you do. Can you identify any by name?

4. Change and growth never come easily, even when things are healthy to start with. What real or potential hurdles might keep your church from greater health and impact?

5. What are some opportunities in which you could share your heart with others from your church, both formally and informally? How could you instigate such discussion?

ACTION STEPS

1. Take some time right now to pray and ask God to guide you through a personal journey of rediscovery, reaffirmation, and rekindled passion for his desires. Talk to him about your church. Praise him for all he has done, is doing,

and will do in your fellowship. Ask him to use you to help shape its future.

2. Who are some non-Christians with whom you have or could build a genuine relationship? Which of these people do you have the greatest burden for right now? How might you spend some quality time with one or two of them in the next couple of weeks? Begin to pray daily for them, their circumstances, their needs, and for opportunities to spend time together.

3. Write the words of Matthew 28:18-20 on a three-by-five card, carry it in your pocket or purse, and review it daily until you have learned it by heart.

WELL AFTER ALL, HE DID SAY "I'LL MAKE YOU FISHERS WITH MEN"...DIDN'T HE?

Carrying the Torch

The great commission: one paragraph of Scripture aptly named to describe the fundamental mandate Jesus gave his followers. One driving purpose handed to every generation of believers since the birth of the church. One mandate given to us intact nearly two thousand years after the words originally left his lips. We stand in our position now at the end of a chain that stretches back directly to Jesus. Think of it like the chain of torch bearers just prior to the Summer Olympics.

Every four years the Summer Olympics begins with an event that captures the imagination of the world: the lighting of the Olympic flame. At the end of an international marathon relay, one final runner enters the Olympic stadium. After traveling by foot over thousands of miles, the torchbearer enters the stadium and, to the thrill of millions, ignites the enormous Olympic flame.

Wouldn't it be exciting to be one of those runners, those bearers of the flame? Can you imagine holding that piece of tradition in your hands and knowing that for a brief moment you were the link in that historic chain?

Picture it. Each stride throbs with a sense of mission. Your fingers trace the shape and sculpture of this forged symbol of Olympic competition. All fatigue fades before the once-in-a-lifetime adrenaline of the moment. Your experience would be a family legend. Grandkids would point out your picture to their friends and boast, "See that picture? That's my grandpa (or grandma) there. He carried the torch to the Olympics!"

As Christians, we carry a torch.

We carry a flame of so much greater value that there is no comparison. The pomp and circumstance of the Olympics pales against the eternal significance of the ministry given to us by Christ. Contrast the picturesque image of proud Olympic runners and global applause with the reality of Christians bearing the torch of the gospel through centuries of persecution and trial. The flame we carry is not a symbol, but the light of the gospel needed by a dark and dying world.

These are days for the church of Christ to strengthen our grip on the torch we carry and lift it high. They are days for believers to run with passion and pride because of the Good News in Christ. It is time for us to run with purpose and meaning, tenaciously, because the days are dark and the time may be short.

There is no better way to rediscover passion for the ministry we've been given than to return to the point when Jesus first passed on the torch. Understanding what he said in that pivotal moment will enable us to carry on the ministry of Christ as he intended us to. It will set us free and fuel our spirits.

THE ORIGINAL HANDOFF

Matthew records these words at the very end of his Gospel. They were probably some of Jesus' last words to his disciples.

After his ascension, when they could no longer see nor hear him, these words were left ringing in their ears. Matthew accomplishes the same feat for us with an ingenious stroke of the pen. Long after we have closed the pages of his Gospel, we are still mulling over the challenge Jesus left his original followers. The finale of Matthew's masterpiece is the clarion call of the church. We have traditionally entitled this passage the great commission. But the very word *great* may terrify us, or make us uncomfortable. It's easy for us to think that talking to others about Christ is meant to be done by those who are trained in spiritual matters: pastors or elders. *I can't do that,* you think. *Not little ol' me. I'd mess it up.*

But let's take a close look at what happens in Matthew. It was a day of graduation. A day for the handoff. From the very beginning, Jesus had told his disciples of his desire to make them "fishers of men." He had involved them in ministry. He had taught them his priorities and allowed them to observe him in action. But things were different now. Knowing that the time for his ascension was near, he called them together and spoke these compelling words:

> *All authority in heaven and on earth has been given to me. Therefore go and make disciples of all nations, baptizing them in the name of the Father and of the Son and of the Holy Spirit, and teaching them to obey everything I have commanded you. And surely I am with you always, to the very end of the age.*
> Matthew 28:18-20

As monumental as this proclamation was, it came as no surprise. These words were given to men who had walked with Jesus through every conceivable circumstance of life. He didn't live life one way and charge his followers to live another. He had walked, talked, and breathed these priorities and principles before their eyes. It would be impossible to summarize his life more concisely. The great commission was a summary statement of his passion, his purpose, his lifestyle.

Within those few words is an autobiographical description of the driving priorities of Jesus' life. You could call this the mission statement of his life, and now it is given to his disciples.

It made perfect sense. Peter, James, John—they all knew immediately what Jesus was saying. He was handing his ministry to them and commissioning them to continue doing what he had done. He was expressing the same thought he had said to them earlier, "As the Father has sent me, I am sending you" (John 20:21). He was counting on them to walk as he had walked. They accepted his challenge and turned their world upside down. And now they have passed on the same mandate to you and me.

Jesus told them earlier to take up their cross and follow him. Now, here, in this pivotal paragraph, he identifies what it means to follow him. Following Christ means living the way Jesus lived. It means living by the same priorities, following the same principles, and developing the same patterns. In Jesus' mind, this is the *normal* Christian life.

Why are Jesus' words that were so clear to those men so foggy and confusing to us? How can a moving, life-changing, unforgettable, passionate conversation with Christ be so humdrum to us today? Why are we so often searching for ministry secrets everywhere else and missing the brilliance of this simple commission given by Christ? It is time to restore a passion for the great commission to the heart of the local church. It is time for us to walk, talk, breathe, and even sweat the priorities given by Christ in this commission. It is time to reclaim the great commission as the normal pattern for every follower of Christ: the everyday commission. To do so, we'll have to clear away some of the confusion that has developed.

UNDOING A GREAT CONFUSION

Learning to understand and live by the principles of the great commission demands that we confront the confusion that surrounds it. At least four misleading perspectives have diluted our understanding of, as well as the power of, the great commission.

Confusing Perspective #1:
The great commission is a special command for special Christians, or "real disciples."

When the great commission speaks of "disciples," many Christians breathe a sigh of relief, believing they are justly ruled out. We think of disciples as people who stand spiritually head and shoulders above the rest of us. We think they are far more dedicated, disciplined, diligent, prayerful, knowledgeable, and spiritual than "normal" Christians.

Although we wouldn't use the term, we tend to believe only *super-Christians* attain the status of *disciple*. Most Christians recognize the weaknesses of their faith and inconsistencies of their lifestyle. Therefore, in their own eyes, they believe they are only "normal" believers and can never hope to become "disciples." As a result, they believe the great commission must not apply to them. After all, how could anyone dare to "make disciples" of others if they have no hope of ever becoming one themselves?

Through the logic of this confused perspective, the great commission has been stripped of all relevance and power. The blazing flame to be carried with boldness into a desperate world becomes a flicker carried with apology and excuse. It is hard to fuel a passion for outreach in the local church if most believers cannot see themselves in these words.

Before going any further, evaluate your own thinking. Have you fallen prey to this myth? Tell yourself the truth! A disciple is not a super-Christian. Disciples are simply people who have committed themselves to follow and become like their Master. The term *disciple* was used of people in many religious movements to describe those who followed a religious leader. Therefore, *disciple* was the common term for all followers of Christ until the label *Christian* was first used in Antioch (Acts 11:26). There is nothing complex or mysterious about it. A disciple of Christ is a person who has decided to follow Jesus and desires to become like him. *Disciple* is a term that applies to every believer. And just as *disciple* refers to every true believer, so the great commission is Jesus' mandate for every believer—the pattern of the normal Christian life.

Dallas Willard, in *Spirit of the Disciplines* (New York: Harper & Row, 1988, 258), says it this way:

> *The word "disciple" occurs 269 times in the New Testament. "Christian" is found only three times and was first introduced to refer precisely to disciples. . . . The disciple of Jesus is not the deluxe or heavy-duty model of the Christian—especially padded, textured, streamlined, and empowered for the fast lane on the straight and narrow way. He stands on the pages of the New Testament as the first level of basic transportation in the Kingdom of God.*

Confusing Perspective #2:
The great commission describes a call to missions.

The first phrase of the great commission is responsible for this viewpoint—"Go and make disciples of all nations." This phrase jumps out and compels us to think of Jesus' global agenda. Acts 1:8 expands on this by speaking in terms of being "my witnesses in Jerusalem, and in all Judea and Samaria, and to the ends of the earth." But notice that fulfilling the great commission begins in our Jerusalem, then Judea and Samaria, and finally to the ends of the earth. Missions is eventually a part of the great commission, but it doesn't start there.

We are so accustomed to viewing this as a missions text that some reading this page will bristle at the mere suggestion of an alternative. Hear us out. You'll see that, without minimizing the cross-cultural work of missionaries at all, this phrase really describes a way of life for every believer. It calls all of us to a missions mindset for all of life.

Confusing Perspective #3:
The great commission is a call to evangelism.

Sure, it emphasizes evangelism. But not to the exclusion of the other priorities in Jesus' ministry. When we look at Christ's life, we do see the priority of evangelism, but that emphasis is balanced with a continual emphasis on extended times alone with his disciples.

In Mark 6:31 Jesus tells his disciples, "Come with me by yourselves to a quiet place and get some rest." In Mark 7:24 it says, "Jesus left that place and went to the vicinity of Tyre [a resort-like region]. He entered a house and did not want anyone to know it." Why? To spend time establishing and equipping the disciples in their faith. In Mark 9:30-31, Jesus clearly lays out his balanced priorities when "they left that place and passed through Galilee. Jesus did not want anyone to know where they were, because he was teaching his disciples."

With the best of motives, we preachers have used this hallmark passage to encourage evangelism. Some see any other activity in this text as a lesser priority. However, just as the lifestyle of Jesus demonstrates a balance of disciple-building priorities, so does the mandate of the great commission.

Confusing Perspective #4:
The great commission calls us to highly structured
discipleship training.

Discipleship has become a loaded and overused term. Generally it is regarded as a process of highly structured study where a more mature believer imparts to a younger believer a wide range of biblical essentials. Intense study and accountability are used to impart knowledge and skills for Christian living and ministry. This emphasis misses the balance of the great commission by implying that disciples are special believers and thus this passage is something less than all-inclusive.

In all of this confusion we have swindled the great commission out of its clout. We have created competition among the different aspects of this single command to make disciples. We have created a situation in which the people of Christ are confused and unsure how to carry on the work of Christ, even if they can. We must find the courage to go against the grain of popular understanding and reclaim the clarity inherent in this passage.

Two months after I (Gary) came to my present church, we were to have a missions emphasis series. It was decided that this would be an ideal time for me to present a message on my vision for our church locally and for our involvement globally. I jumped at the chance.

I chose to tackle this challenge with a message based on the great commission. I went to great lengths to express the fact that the great commission is just as much God's agenda for individual believers in their own neighborhoods as it is for missionaries entering new cultures. Jesus calls each of us to bring the gospel to the people in our corner of the world and help them grow as followers of Christ who are in turn equipped to reach their corner of the world. The message went well, and the people of my church began thinking about what God was calling them to do within their own everyday sphere of influence.

The following Sunday a missionary came as a guest speaker. His assignment was to challenge our people to consider the needs of those without Christ in other cultures. So far, so good.

Stepping up to the podium, he opened his Bible and began his remarks. "Go ye into all the world and make disciples!" He stopped there and paused for effect, satisfied the entire point of the great commission had been conveyed in that one phrase. (As a matter of fact, he felt that the first two words of the King James translation were enough.) "Jesus commanded us, 'Go ye!'" he said. And for the thirty minutes he harangued my people with the need to go cross-culturally in order to fulfill the great commission. In his mind, the sum total of the great commission was found in the words "Go ye." He taught that the great commission calls us to go somewhere else, that to do less was second best.

You can imagine the confusion that resulted. The thinking prompted by the first message was diluted and derailed of any urgency. The confusion experienced by my people crippled their confidence about stepping out with conviction.

It is time to return to the actual words of Jesus and allow him to ignite his passion within us.

BACK TO THE SOURCE

Understanding the great commission is really simple. Regardless of whether you've never looked closely at these famous statements, or you have covered this ground recently, let's take a few minutes to review what Jesus actually said.

The heart of the great commission is one command explained by three participial phrases. Don't panic. This is not going to be a grammar lesson, but understanding some key grammatical aspects of this passage will help you understand the passage accurately.

The only command of this passage is to *make disciples.* Literally, the first phrase says, "As you are going, make disciples." That's it. Though most of us have heard different preachers elevate one of the phrases in this passage above the others, the command to make disciples is the central and only imperative of the great commission. Everything else in this passage revolves around the axis of this one command to make disciples.

A loose paraphrase of the great commission might give you better perspective: As you are *going* throughout the world [anywhere and everywhere during the course of your lives], *make disciples* [as a matter of habit, lifestyle, and constant priority], *baptizing* people who choose to follow me [as part of the process of establishing them in their faith]. And make it your habit to be *teaching* them to observe all of the things I have worked to teach you [equipping them to carry on these very priorities in their lives, obeying and serving me fully].

Do you see it? Can you sense the way each aspect of this passage explains the process of fulfilling the one command? Did you recognize the way each part is integrated together to form a full-circle process? When you see the central place of the command to make disciples and the manner in which the other phrases bring it to life, the whole passage takes on new clarity.

"As you are going" tells us that this command is not a specialized concept for a new program, but a matter of lifestyle. Wherever you live, no matter what you do for a living, this command of Christ calls all of us who are his followers to be reaching those who are lost. It calls us to pattern our lives after his, to be his personal emissaries into each sphere of influence where God has placed us. This phrase describes the lifestyle of continually working to win people to Christ.

"Baptizing them" is obviously a reference to the formal act publicly demonstrating a person's decision to follow Christ. But beneath the surface, baptism conveys much more. In the culture of Jesus' day, baptism was an external expression of an internal belief system and was practiced by religious groups. It showed the progress of growth in a disciple's life as he or she took a public step to become more established in faith. Baptism played an important part in helping people who had come to Christ take the next step of confirming and expressing their new identity in Christ. It reflected their desire to become rooted in the basics of their faith. For us, this phrase compells us to help people become rooted and built up in their faith after they have come to salvation in Christ. It means winning *and* building

"Teaching them to obey" is the process of equipping people to put their faith into action. A disciple is one who chooses to follow his master and desires to become like him. Teaching people to obey what Jesus taught is helping them live the way he did, to walk as Jesus walked, in every area of life. Equipping goes beyond teaching someone the Bible. It involves developing skills, attitudes, and actions consistent with the life of Christ. It includes equipping people to make disciples of their own peers.

Jesus commissioned his followers to follow his own model. He wanted his disciples to help others become fully devoted followers, just as he had helped them. This means the disciples were to do among their peers what Jesus had done in their lives. If they succeeded, those they helped would in turn do the same in the lives of others, who would continue to do the same until he returned.

Maybe you already catch the moving dynamics of these words. They cover the entire process of making disciples: winning, building, and equipping. This process begins when we go to where people are, bring them to Christ, ground them in him, and equip them to share Christ and his love with others. There is an undeniable feeling of balance. Nothing dominates to the exclusion of other priorities.

Any approach to the great commission that emphasizes one aspect above the rest shortchanges the whole. Any approach that misses the everyman nature of these principles misses the heart of Jesus. Christ's desire was to replicate his drive, his priorities, his lifestyle, and his character in the lives of his followers. Those who would follow him would live as he did.

This everyday commission calls us to reach our own peers for Christ. It calls us to follow the priorities of Jesus wherever God has placed us.

PICK UP THE TORCH

Ron, Alan, and the members of their church had lost sight of the mandate they had been given. In many ways they were running hard, but they had lost sight of where they were headed. Their feet were moving and they were working up a sweat, but to what end? It was time for renewed passion and purpose—time to grab hold of the torch, time to regain an accurate sense of calling. Christ's everyday commission is that calling. It is the substance of our passion.

In that timeless moment, Jesus challenged us to a lifestyle of making disciples among those God brings into our lives. For a teenager, it may be other teenagers. For young adults, it may include neighbors and work associates. For senior citizens, it may be those in the neighborhood or senior citizens' home where they live. He called us to be passionate about reaching our peers, establishing them in their faith, and helping them duplicate the process in the lives of their peers.

We stand in that continuous chain of believers that began with the first disciples. We have received the very same torch Jesus personally handed to them. It is as if the words of the great commission were spoken as distinctly to us as they were to the disciples. So let them speak to you. Allow his passion to become yours. Allow his desire to become your desire. Recognize the fact that just like every believer before you, you have been placed in your community to fulfill the mission of Christ in your generation.

CHAPTER 2

QUESTIONS FOR REFLECTION

1. In this chapter, we discussed some of the common perceptions of the great commission. Which are most prevalent among the people of your church? If you were to guess, what percentage of the people at your church would say that the focus of the great commission is missions? Evangelism? Discipleship? Teaching? How many would have no idea?

2. Those perceptions have shaped our values as a Christian community for quite some time, and values resist change. Which view do you think is the hardest to change? Why?

3. We have examined the great commission as a prescription for the normal Christian life—the pattern of life we were

recreated for—but for many, this emphasis is new. How would you describe the priorities and patterns of the normal Christian life as you have been taught to understand it?

4. How comfortable would most people in your church be referring to themselves as disciples? How comfortable would you be referring to yourself as a disciple? Which aspect of the discussion about the term *disciple* in this chapter do you think carries the most weight for convincing people to view their position in Christ differently?

5. Maintaining balance is nearly impossible; at any given moment we are out of balance. Yet when you look at the overall pattern of your life, how balanced are the three priorities of winning, building, and equipping? Which priority usually gets the most attention? Which gets the least? What factors in life make balance difficult for you? Can you think of someone who might work with you so that the two of you could help each other balance these priorities?

FOR FURTHER STUDY

1. Spend time reflecting on the life and ministry of Christ. Try to identify times when you can recognize him intentionally winning (reaching out to help people come to know him as Savior), building (establishing his followers in their faith), and equipping (training men and women to evangelize and care for their peers).

2. Identify events and passages in the rest of the New Testament where you can see the apostles and the early church following the same pattern.

Personal Implications

Picturesque waterfalls capture our imagination. Perhaps that's why they grace the cover of travel brochures and fill volumes of vacation photos. There are few, if any, more inviting images.

Imagine, for a moment, you are standing beneath one of those tropical waterfalls. The water tumbles over the rocks above, dancing off your shoulders into the pristine pool at your feet. Its rhythmic rumbling drowns out all other noise and all reminders of the world. You stand there under the water, momentarily enveloped in a private little soundproof, stress-proof world. Its gentle warmth and massaging pulse make it hard to step away.

Good. Stay right there. Only allow the water rinsing over you to be the great commission. Feel its impact. Listen to its message. Linger there. Allow the significance of Jesus' words to capture your undivided attention and come alive for you in a new way.

For the rest of this book, we will linger directly under the flow of that watershed passage, the great commission. We will allow it to soak us, refresh us, and rekindle a burning passion for the work of Christ. We will find its simple purity motivating, as well as challenging. And we'll consider how we might invite others to discover its life-changing implications.

We begin with a look at the personal implications. In the following chapters we will address implications for the church, and then implications on a national or global scale. For now we will zero in on the personal level, where each of us lives.

THINKING IN PERSONAL TERMS

It's no secret; our generation looks to institutions to solve the problems that plague us. When it comes to the needs of mankind or problems of society, we expect to find institutional solutions. When it comes to the work of Christ, we expect the church to do it. This causes us to believe that such an important work as the great commission must naturally fall to the church or missions organizations, rather than individuals.

Yet, as we have already seen, this commission was given to each of us. Followers of Christ have been given the mandate to reach the people within their own sphere of influence. As we are going through life, we are called to make disciples of those God brings into our lives on a regular basis.

That means junior-highers reaching junior-highers, high-school students reaching other high-school students, young adults reaching young adults, senior citizens reaching senior citizens, teachers reaching teachers, police officers reaching police officers. . . . Can you sense the potential for penetrating an entire generation together?

I (Dann) live in a subdivision of ninety-five homes. Christ's everyday commission both demands and gives me the privilege and joy of partnering with God in reaching those ninety-five homes for Christ. My neighbors have become my friends, my peers—those whom God has brought into my life. It is not my pastor's job to share Christ's love with those neighbors—it is my responsibility and privilege. My pastor does not live in that neighborhood—I do! In the same way, your pastor cannot reach your peers, because they are not his peers. He has no relationship with them. He does not know the needs in their lives that may serve as windows for the gospel. He has no history with them, no credibility as someone who genuinely cares for them. But you do! And the primary vehicle God uses to reach someone for Christ is a caring relationship with a genuine believer.

Your church is hampered by the same limitations facing your pastor. The body of Christ to which you belong can assist you by providing programs and tools to help you reach your peers, but your church cannot reach your peers. Your peers are only connected with the ministry of your church through you. You are a God-ordained conduit through which they might discover new life in Christ and then become connected with the church. Your relationship with them is a redemptive bridge across which they can meet Jesus.

In a generation that is skeptical of religious institutions, it is people, not steeples, that will point others to Christ.

YOUR PERSONAL MISSION FIELD

Who are the people God has brought into your life who don't know Christ?

Think about them for a moment. They may regularly come through your door at work. They may live next door or down the street. They may share a class with you in school. They may be seated beside you on the bleachers at your child's little league game. They may be coworkers with whom you share coffee breaks. They may be in the restaurant you frequent for lunch, or the garage where you take your car. They may be relatives, and may even live under your own roof. They may be anywhere. Together they form your sphere of influence. They are the mission field into which God has planted you. Be careful not to walk by them.

Jesus illustrated the way God brings people into our lives with a pointed, even uncomfortable, story. Here's a loose paraphrase. One man visiting town on business was mugged, badly injured, and robbed of everything he had. His attackers left him, abused and tossed aside, slumped helplessly on the sidewalk, in desperate need. People from town who had witnessed this travesty refused to help and quickly walked away.

Naturally, a few passersby would soon respond to the severity of this traveler's need—at least you would expect them to. But none did. Until finally one man stopped to help—the ungodly one you'd least expect! You know the story. In Jesus' version, only a Samaritan felt compelled to get involved. A priest and a Levite stepped to the other side of the road in order to escape the need of this traveler (Luke 10:30-37).

Jesus' point? Open your eyes and recognize those God has brought into your life. Look for those already in your path, whom you can serve as a genuine neighbor—those who need Christ and his redemptive love, regardless of how they look to society. Those with whom you share interests, work, sports, anything. Anyone whom God has brought into your life qualifies as your neighbor.

We all feel a great temptation to choose safety and freedom from risk, to avoid involvement. However, the great commission challenges us to get personally involved in bringing people to Christ, establishing them in their faith, and then equipping them to share their faith with their peers.

Jesus understood how easy it is for us to walk past the obvious. He understood that it seems more glorious to travel to exotic destinations to fulfill the great commission. He knew that special outreach and ministry programs that take us into "foreign territory" sound exciting. But he also knew that around the corner, down the hallway at work, is a world of hurting people, desperate for the work of Christ—your mission field.

These people in your life need to see the Savior at work in the life of a real person. With the relentless bashing of the church in the media, people are skeptical about trusting the message of Christianity. They see religious zealots on street corners downtown. They hear news of scandals involving religious leaders. They see the proliferation of movements, cults, and Eastern religious groups and find very little that compels them to consider Christ.

You are the window through which they see the truth about Christ. Living out the great commission on an everyday, personal level means taking responsibility to build redemptive relationships with your peers.

STRATEGY FOR A LIFETIME

Integrate the principles of this everyday commission into your life and you'll find a strategy for living that will last a lifetime. Here is a pattern worth duplicating and sharpening throughout your life, a lifestyle that will make an impact that can never be erased. It applies to every believer at every stage of their life.

We have a tendency to make simple things difficult, complicated, to depend on experts. Yet the great commission is a simple call to all believers to invest their lives in winning, building, and equipping.

One key is making it a priority to meet people at their place of need and then balancing the priorities of winning the lost, building the believer, and equipping the workers. Together these priorities give your life deep roots and help you bear real fruit. Practicing this strategy is simply a matter of making regular decisions on three levels.

Priority #1: Winning

Make relationships with non-Christians a priority in your life. Sadly, most Christians who have been following Christ for very long have very few significant relationships with non-believers. Identify and maintain a mental list of the non-Christian friends whom you would most like to see come to Christ. Plan time for them in your schedule. Find ways to expose them to other believers with interests similar to their own. And pray for them constantly. You might find that keeping a list of your "most wanted" on a card in your Bible keeps you focused on this priority.

Priority #2: Building

Continually participate in those activities that will help you grow roots to your faith. Place yourself in environments and relationships that will build you up in your faith. Make sure that you are always involved in things that increase your understanding of God, his work, his Word, and his Son. Just as Psalm 1 speaks of the flourishing tree planted by the stream, choose to plant your life next to those sources of instruction and nurture that will cause your faith to flourish. Keep meeting together with other believers to grow deeper in your knowledge of him.

Priority #3: Equipping

Share your insights and experiences in reaching out to your peers with others. When you see one of your friends come to Christ, help them learn to reach their peers. In the great commission, Jesus told us to "teach them to observe all I have commanded you." Teaching people to observe means teaching them to serve their peers. It also requires the choice to share what God has been doing in your life. Equipping another person to reach their peers means opening up and letting them learn from the ways God has taught you. Identify key individuals God has brought into your life and spend extra time with them—to share your life with them. Paul speaks of this priority in 1 Thessalonians 2:8, where he says, "We loved you so much that we were delighted to share with you not only the gospel of God but our lives as well, because you had become so dear to us."

When you begin to understand that such a profound strategy is merely a matter of simple choices, you can sense the beauty of Jesus' words in a very personal way. This powerful lifestyle has nothing to do with ministry title, career path, income level, age, education, family circumstances, or any other circumstantial factor. You can live your life by these priorities no matter who you are. You can invest your life meaningfully in the lives of others and make an impact that lasts for eternity.

Why not take a little personal inventory right now? Are you routinely involved in activities that are sending your spiritual roots deeper, or have you begun to take those things for granted?

Do you have a few non-Christian friends with whom you are building redemptive relationships? Are you looking for or creating ways to expose them to Christ, the church, and Christians in a positive way?

And have you prioritized people with whom you are investing your life, sharing the lessons of ministry and outreach you have learned? Do you regularly discuss with others the things God has taught you about reaching your peers? Have you tried teaming up together to reach out to unbelieving peers?

OBEDIENCE OR OPPORTUNITY?

As you begin to understand these personal implications of the everyday commission fully, you begin to recognize a double-barreled motivation to action. On the one hand, it's a matter of obedience. Every believer with a tender heart is eager to please the Lord through obedience, and the great commission is clearly a command to be obeyed. Therefore the words of Jesus are enough of a motivation for most of us. If he commanded it, we reason, we will do our best to live by it.

On the other hand, there is a sense of opportunity that permeates the principles of the great commission. Here, in simple terms, is a description of how we might live by the same priorities as Christ. Here is the pattern that the disciples learned from Jesus and then followed as they turned the world upside down. It's all right there for us to follow. It is an opportunity to live the way Jesus lived and participate in the same work of the kingdom that we observe in his life.

In an age when people struggle for a sense of significance, the great commission gives us a *why* for our lives. It inspires a reason to live. It is the ultimate cause and worthy of our deepest passions. It conveys a prescription for living life as an investment in the eternal. It identifies a lifelong strategy for making a mark that cannot be erased. It is not just a strategy for pastors or missionaries; it is for you, for every aspect of your life.

We all long to make our lives really count for something. And, if we understand the great commission, that craving can be genuinely satisfied. Jesus gave us the key to making our

lives count in the greatest possible way. The chance to participate in the heart of his work is one of the greatest privileges
and most profound opportunities of life.

All that Jesus accomplished in the lives of his followers
was done in about three years. Can you imagine how much
could be accomplished for the kingdom by people who live
by these priorities all their lives?

How many years of active adult life do you have left?
Assuming typical life expectancy, you might have ten, twenty,
thirty, or many more years. The significance of the opportunity before you is staggering. The impact of your obedience
might be reflected in this comment of Jesus to his disciples
just before his death: "Anyone who has faith in me will do
what I have been doing. He will do even greater things than
these" (John 14:12).

Our work is not greater in quality or greater in importance.
Nothing we do could ever be greater in essence than the work
of Christ. But it is very possible that Jesus knew we would
have a chance to accomplish more in terms of making disciples during our lifetime than he did in the brevity of his. Jesus
had three years in which to make disciples; we have thirty-
plus years. What a privilege!

Recognize the opportunity to invest your energy in the
eternal. Begin to filter the decisions and direction of your life
through these principles. Rather than pursuing the inevitable
career path, evaluate job opportunities in light of your everyday commission priorities and involvements. Does one job
keep you more involved with unbelievers than another? How
does a potential move affect your sphere of influence? As you
pursue your hobbies, is there a way to involve those on your
most-wanted list? Do the choices you make help or hinder
your great commission balance?

In short, allow great commission priorities to affect the tangible decisions of your life on a daily basis. Make the simple choices it takes to make the greatest possible impact in your sphere of influence for as long as God allows you to be there.

YEAH, BUT . . .

Time for a reality check!

Any new venture or change in direction brings with it a new set of hurdles to be conquered. This process of applying the principles of the great commission to our lives is no exception. Regardless of how much you would like to reach the people God has placed in your life, you will likely find a hurdle standing in your way. Regardless of how much passion this discussion fires up in you, there is probably a "Yeah, but . . ." growing in your thoughts.

For most people, what gets in the way is a fear of not having much to offer. Just as we believe that "disciples" are Christians on a whole different plane of maturity and effectiveness, we also tend to believe that ordinary, run-of-the-mill believers have little to offer. We find it hard to believe that God really would or could use us to change the lives of others. We fear we don't know enough or won't have the right answers. We are crippled by the notion that we have too many flaws, too much "junk" in our lives. For one reason or another, a great many of us feel like we have so much to work on in our own lives that there is no point in pretending we have something to offer someone else.

At the bottom of it all is a devious lie, which says, "I have to impress people with myself if I want them to be impressed with Jesus." Don't believe that for a minute. No one of us is the Savior; he is. We don't hold the key to new life; he does. We are not ever going to be perfect; he is perfect. We don't earn our salvation; he earned it for us. We can't provide all the answers; he is the answer.

In spite of the messages we are accustomed to telling ourselves, reaching out to our peers can be simple. And God is eager to use regular people like us in a supernatural way.

Peter and John were going up to the temple at the time of daily prayer. Nothing special, just two regular guys joining the crowd for a daily occurrence. On their way into the temple, they saw a man crippled from birth, sitting in his regular spot, begging for alms. It was his ordinary activity being conducted in the ordinary way at his ordinary spot. However, today would be anything but ordinary.

When Peter and John met the beggar's gaze, Peter said, "Silver or gold I do not have, but what I have I give you. In the name of Jesus Christ of Nazareth, walk" (Acts 3:6). And the crippled man got up and danced away into the temple courts.

Our temptation is to believe that we must possess impressive gifts and abilities. Without something impressive to rely on, what kind of impact can we hope to make in the lives of others? In the words of Peter, we have no silver and gold to offer. The truth is, we are sinful, flawed people—but we have found Christ, and that changes everything.

The one genuine gift we have to offer we possess in abundance. The greatest need of the world is the one we are able to meet. We can say with Peter, "I may not have impressive credentials, polished answers, an unblemished background, a perfect marriage, or even a dramatic personal testimony, but I have Jesus. And more than anything in all the world I would love to give him to you."

When you find yourself afraid you have little to offer, remember what you do have. You have Jesus. And you have all the authority of Christ behind every step you take to live by the priorities of his everyday commission.

CHAPTER 3

QUESTIONS FOR REFLECTION

1. What are some of the ways we expect the church as an institution or pastors in particular to be responsible for carrying out the work of the great commission?

2. Why is it so hard for us to reach out to our own peers and friends who do not know Christ? Be as specific as you can, and list as many reasons as you can think of.

3. If it's hard for you to reach out to your unbelieving peers, it is probably tough for other believers, too. How might you team up with friends to help one another begin reaching unbelieving friends for Christ?

4. Let's try to define your sphere of influence, your personal corner of the "mission field." First, brainstorm on paper. Try to flesh out your understanding of your potential spheres of influence in the following areas, and then ask yourself who some of the specific people in that sphere of your life might be.

Community

Neighborhood

Job/Career

Hobbies

Clubs/Associations

Children's Interests

Now try to summarize your thoughts. In your own words, rewrite Acts 1:8 to reflect the spheres of influence God has given you.

5. Imagine that you received a tempting job offer. How might your role in your current sphere of influence affect your decision-making process?

6. Finally, complete the following sentence: "*Yeah,* it makes sense, and I would like to be involved in winning the lost, building the believers, and equipping my peers to follow and serve Christ, *but . . .*"

OBVIOUSLY NOT A VERY GROWTH
MINDED CONGREGATION ...

Churchwide Implications

Ron, Alan, and our friends from chapter 1 reflect a gnawing concern among many in the church today. While we have grown skilled at the management of ministry, the raising of funds, the education of clergy, and the writing of curriculum, we grope hungrily for secrets of restoring the heart of Christ and substance of his ministry to the local church. We long for the passion and focus of the early church. We eagerly hope to be instrumental in a national revival such as we have never seen. We are burdened by the needs of the lost world surrounding us, yet our honorable desires run headlong into the crushing reality of the church's declining impact.

The edifice of Christianity in America stands intact, but the influence of our ministry is tumbling downhill at a frightening pace. A quick look at a few statistics will heighten your sense of urgency for the mission, the challenge facing our churches.

■ There are approximately 350,000 Protestant churches in America.

Of these churches, 65 percent have plateaued or are declining in attendance: "One third of all traditional churches in the world today plateau at 50 members. Another third quit growing when there are 150 members. Twenty-eight percent will stop growing when there are 350 members. Only 5 percent grow larger than this, and most plateau at 1,000 or 2,000."

Ralph Neighbor, *Where Do We Go from Here?*

Of the churches that are growing in America, 85 percent of that growth has been by people who church-hop (transfer growth).

Chuck Colson, *The Body*

■ It takes the average evangelical church one year and one hundred members to introduce one person to Christ.

Bob Gilliam Church Development Survey,
quoted by Bill Hull in *Can We Save
the Evangelical Church?*

■ In 1963, 65 percent of Americans said they believed in the absolute truth of all the words in the Bible. Within fifteen years, by 1978, this had declined to 38 percent, and is now at 32 percent.

PRRC Emerging Trends, January 1992;
see also Colson, *The Body*

■ In one region of North America, a group of churches calculated that it cost them over a year's work and $19,008 for every person they saw come to Christ.

Don Hodgins, Church Growth Consultant, Canada

"How can this be true?" you ask. "We are working so hard!" "We care about the lost. We are striving for greater effectiveness. We haven't given up."

You are probably thinking of your own church, where dozens or even hundreds of people work hard every week to see that the ministry is healthy. You might be feeling a little defensive, worried that we are about to criticize your church's ministry. On the contrary, it is our assumption that the very reason you are reading this book is because of your deep love for Christ and your passion and desire to see your ministry thrive.

This chapter on the church makes no attempt to present some magic curriculum. Rather, we just want to step back underneath the waterfall and allow the principles of the great commission to wash over the church. We'll keep our focus there, because the great commission contains the heart of our calling. It offers purpose and the clear simplicity of refreshing principles for the local church.

THE GREAT COMMISSION IN FOCUS

We have looked at length at the great commission and its implications for each of us. We have seen that the great commission summarizes the lifestyle of Jesus. We have learned that it calls us to live as he did. It challenges us to believe that the pattern of the normal Christian life is to walk as he did, to follow the same priorities he lived. We discovered that Jesus intended for every believer to be involved in winning, building, and equipping others to live as his disciples. In this way the great commission invites each of us to discover the ultimate life of significance as we follow him.

However, how does a local church follow and facilitate the mandate of the great commission? In light of the fact that the great commission was given to individuals, not just institutions, where does the local church fit in?

Just as the church does not exist independently of individual Christians, so individual Christians are never abandoned to go it alone either. God ordained the local church to help believers successfully carry out the work of the great commission among their peers.

As you have been called to win your peers to Christ, build them up in their faith, and equip them to duplicate the same process, your church has been ordained to support, equip, assist, and encourage you and every member of your church in your efforts to make disciples of your peers.

If we depend on anything else to help people carry out the work, we have abdicated our responsibility as the local body of Christ. We have been brought together to help one another.

In some ways, this book and this chapter in particular are meant to serve as a wake-up call for the church. It is time for us to reclaim the full scope of the ministry that Jesus gave us. It is time for us to reconsider how we might more effectively help people succeed in making disciples of their peers. It is time to restore a passion for the great commission to the heart of the local church.

IMPACT ON PROGRAMS

The pattern of the great commission does not demand that we maintain a zillion programs, but it calls us to do a few things well. It calls us to model corporately the balance and simplicity we would like to see in the lives of individuals in our churches. Being busy does not necessarily make a church effective any more than being a busy person makes you an effective person. Nor is a large church necessarily more effective than a small one. What matters is an intentional and balanced effort to help people succeed in living out the priorities of the great commission.

What should those programs look like? How does a church structure its programming to help people successfully make disciples of their peers? By now you can probably guess. The answer is simply to focus on the three priorities of winning, building, and equipping. If these priorities form the pattern for healthy Christian living, they also identify the purposes that must drive our programs.

WINNING PRIORITIES

A church that understands Christ's everyday commission will work hard to structure outreach events that are designed to help people expose their unsaved peers to Christ, his church, and Christians in a positive way. Corporate outreach efforts, however, do not replace personal responsibility. When we begin to work together, this commission ceases to be such a great burden and becomes a great adventure.

If we are going to help people succeed in winning their peers to Christ, we must discover new methods. People apart from Christ in a secular world have many hurdles to cross and many questions. Plus, believers in our churches have a churning aversion to typical evangelistic programming. Dick Innes captures the sentiment of most American Christians in his book *I Hate Witnessing!*

Unbelievers are skeptical of the church, and believers are skeptical of typical evangelistic emphasis. It's quite a predicament and an important arena for study. Let's start with the skepticism and resistance that the secular person has toward Christ and the church. How can we help them trust the message of Christianity?

Studies have shown that a typical non-Christian must get to know several Christians well before he or she will trust the message of Christianity. No longer are we living in a culture that has great respect for the church, the Bible, or Christianity in general. We now must start from scratch in winning others to Christ. We cannot afford the luxury of believing that if we build it—nice building, nice programs, etc.—they will come. People today are not out looking for a church to join and not even aware of what Christ has to offer. Therefore, equipping people to win their peers to Christ is a greater challenge than ever before.

The ability to present the gospel clearly will always be important, but there is more to helping people succeed in reaching their peers than giving them the words of a gospel presentation. They need to know how to start from scratch with someone. They want to know how an ordinary believer can walk an unbelieving friend toward Christ in a sensitive *and effective* manner because guerrilla gospel tactics do not work well in the context of a friendship. Skepticism toward Christianity is demolished in the context of relationship, and then the message of the gospel can be heard through the normal process of conversation.

Learning new methods may be a great challenge, but it can actually be a fun hurdle to tackle. You and your church might discover more joy in making evangelism fun than in applying any other single priority. And this teamwork approach to evangelism is surprisingly simple. Here's how it has been working.

Even before we moved into our home, Char and I (Dann) began praying about the mission field of ninety-five new homes in our development. We belong to a church that provides regular events designed to help expose nonbelievers to Christ, so we knew that, as we worked to reach our new neighbors, regular opportunities would arise to support our personal witness. We were excited about the possibilities, but had no idea how much joy and purpose it would bring.

Not long after we moved in, another family moved into the home across the street. Our new neighbor would need plenty of help in getting settled, and we were eager to develop the friendship.

One Saturday afternoon, as we were talking, our neighbor brought up the problem he was having with his landscaping. Excited about the possible connection, we suggested a landscaper who also just happened to attend our church. This landscaper recognized how he might be able to team up with us to reach our neighbors and intentionally trimmed his profits to get the job and establish a new friendship.

Not much later, our neighbor needed to connect with a new doctor in the area, so we recommended one from our church. He wasn't taking more patients, but was willing to help us befriend our new neighbor, so he readily agreed.

As our friendship developed, I soon realized my new neighbor loved to play basketball, so I helped him connect with a basketball league organized by, guess who, another man from our church. Another new network of friends began to develop for my neighbor.

Finally, as the friendship developed, it seemed natural to invite our neighbors to a special event at church. And guess what he commented on when he got there! "I can't believe how many people I already know at your church!"

Those relationships had created a relational context for the message he would hear. My neighbor's skepticism about church and his guard against Christianity had been lowered through relationships with these other men. Char's relationship with his wife is having the same effect. While my neighbor hasn't given his life to Christ yet, I believe God is actively seeking him—and it's happening through a network of developing Christian friendships. I call this team-effort evangelism—working together, each using our gifts, to strategically help each other reach our peers for Christ.

Can you see this process working in the lives of people in your church? Can you see how the strategy is different from what we have become accustomed to? Can you sense ways the church can provide programs to assist people in the process of reaching their peers? The possibilities for creativity are limitless: sports events, musical programs, parenting seminars, seeker-sensitive services, summer camping, outdoor experiences, holiday programs, neighborhood barbecues. . . . Whatever the people of your church would feel comfortable bringing their non-Christian friends to will work. For further thoughts on this process, see chapters 13–14 of our book *Growing a Healthy Church* (Moody Press, 1991).

Obviously, people have different gifts for ministry and different abilities in communicating their faith, but the pattern of the great commission is that every believer would be involved in winning their peers to Christ. Some people are eyes, some are ears, some are hands, and some are mouthpieces, but all can be involved in helping one another reach their peers for Christ. No one is left out.

BUILDING PRIORITIES

Growth-oriented programs are intentionally designed to help people grow in their faith. They provide places into which you can plug new believers and build them up. Just like the team approach of outreach programs, these are tools that enable us to work as partners with each other to help people grow in their faith.

Helping people grow "spiritual roots" is a healthy way to view this priority. Rather than losing focus with some generic concept of spiritual growth, you will find it beneficial to target three specific kinds of roots:

Biblical/theological roots help people grow in their understanding of God, his Word, the work of Christ, and the doctrines of the faith. These roots provide substance and nutrition for our faith. Christianity is not a matter of having faith in faith, but a relationship with the living God that is founded on the truth of his Word and the reality of the work of Christ. Helping people grow biblical/theological roots means helping them sink their foundations deep into the facts of the faith.

Relational roots help people build networks of supportive relationships with other believers. Scripture is filled with encouragement and instruction about the need for, benefits of, and strength found in relationships between believers. However, these relationships do not happen automatically. Relational roots provide strength and support, but they must be cultivated intentionally.

Experiential roots help people celebrate, affirm, and experience the fullness of their relationship to Christ. These roots provide encouragement and expression to our faith. Powerful worship, personal evangelism, and cross-cultural ministry take people beyond the limitations of their previous experience. We can help people send out deeper roots by helping them expand the depth of their experience in living for Christ.

This team approach is powerful. If in the process of winning someone to Christ, other believers and creative church-sponsored events have been involved, by the time they come to Christ they will already have a network of relationships to make them feel at home. They will be comfortable plugging into church programs that encourage their growth. On the other hand, if only one person is involved in reaching someone for Christ, then becoming involved in the church will require conquering the awkward hurdle of feeling like a stranger. If they have had no contact with the church, then it is very possible that they will still feel uncomfortable about participating in the growth-oriented programs offered by the church. The process of the everyday commission is so natural that when we take a team approach in the local church, we pave the way for new believers to take steps of spiritual growth naturally.

EQUIPPING PRIORITIES

Equipping programs are simply programs designed to equip people to reach and disciple their own peers. Having come to Christ and begun growing roots, learning to effectively win and disciple one's peers completes the circle of disciple making.

Living as a disciple is a never-ending process of growing deeper roots spiritually and bearing fruit in ministry to others. The bridge between the two is the process of being equipped and sharpened for effective ministry. Unfortunately, it seems that in many evangelical churches there is little being done intentionally to equip people for ministry. We want them to succeed in winning their peers to Christ, but we do little to help them in that process. We want them to help others grow in their faith, but we act as if they must learn how by divine inspiration.

Balanced programming that reflects the priorities of the great commission must include all three dimensions of winning, building, and equipping. And when all three priorities are in place they work together in a natural, even beautiful, way. In a church environment where winning your peers to Christ is a normal part of life and a process that everyone shares together, new believers will not need to be prodded into doing the same. They will be eager to reach their peers because they view it as the norm. The more they grow in Christ, the more they will want to "reinvest" the overflow of that growth in others. Outreach events will serve as on-the-job training. Other programs to equip people with skills to help them reach their peers will act as a turbocharger on an engine already running.

Therefore, you will find you don't need a vast multitude of equipping programs. Most equipping can be done on the job. A few well-designed vehicles to help people know what they believe, express those beliefs coherently, and respond to some of the predictable arguments of unbelievers may be enough.

You may want to address one special need: Many Christians have few, if any, relationships with non-Christians. As they have grown in relationship with other Christians, they have pulled away from relationships with non-Christian peers. Some have even thought that as Christians they weren't supposed to be involved with non-Christians anymore. Equipping people to reach their peers may also require helping them learn to rebuild friendships with people who don't know Christ. They need to learn how to be like Jesus, who was a friend of sinners.

Experiment. Be flexible. Do whatever it takes to meet the needs of those who are ready to begin reaching others. And have fun in the process!

THE 87-PERCENT PROBLEM—A MAJOR ROADBLOCK

Change is always tough, and it would be unrealistic to imply that the changes you will want to consider in your church will be painless.

A major roadblock to these changes may be the fact that you have been doing things a certain way for a long time. Programs take on a life of their own, whether or not they still achieve the purpose originally intended. And in the typical church, most of our time and energy is already consumed by existing programs geared for the needs of believers. It's what we call the 87 percent problem.

In my (Dann) doctoral studies, I evaluated one hundred different ministeries which said they were committed to the great commission. I found that eighty-seven of the one hundred had all of their programs targeted to helping believers grow. Very little was specifically designed to help people with the task of reaching their unsaved peers. And even less was planned to equip people with the skills they need for effective peer care and peer evangelism.

Don't take our word for it. Why not do your own little test and see how it is in your church? Draw a line down the center of a piece of paper. On the left, list all of the major programs that occur in your church on a regular basis. When you are done, identify who each program is geared for and what it is designed to do for that person. You will need to stick with the *primary* purpose of each program, not a wish list of possible benefits. List these purposes in the column on the right, next to each program. Be honest; this is not a contest. Hopefully you beat the 87-percent factor, but look carefully. Check to see how much of your programming is primarily designed to help believers grow in Christ.

The great commission implies a very distinct balance of programming. We may excel at building believers, but where is the equipping and the winning? Are we hoping that the people of our church learn to reach their peers as lone rangers, or are we teaming up and equipping them to do so?

Consider this: The time and energy of the people in your church is your greatest resource. However, it is a limited resource. They will never have time for every good idea. There will always be more ideas, more options, and more needs than you will have the time and energy to pursue. And if the time and energy of your people is consumed by current programming, you cannot merely add more. Some things may have to be cut or retooled in order to create a balance of winning, building, and equipping programs.

WHEN IT IS TIME TO EVALUATE

Sooner or later you will need to ask the hard questions of evaluation. You will want to look your ministries square in the face and ask, "Are we being effective in accomplishing the great commission?"

While traditionally we have evaluated successful ministry by the "three *B*s," buildings, bucks, and bodies, it is time for different criteria. Bigger churches are not necessarily more successful by great commission standards, but then neither are smaller churches. Size is irrelevant! What matters is whether people are being won to Christ, built up in their faith, and equipped to win and build their peers.

To that end, we would propose that you evaluate your ministry against the standard of the great commission. Your evaluation will show you where to rejoice and where to retool.

First, measure conversion growth.

Are you seeing people being won to Christ? Is it happening regularly? Conversion growth is not the only measurement of effectiveness, but it is a clear sign of health. It is one of two specific areas in which progress can be quantified.

Second, look to see whether the people of your fellowship are involving themselves in efforts to make disciples of their peers.

Spiritual growth is hard to quantify, but you can chart the movement of people into intentional efforts to reach their peers. Spiritual growth should lead people to the point where the overflow of their heart spills over into ministry. If you are building people up in their faith and equipping them to reach others, then a fair measurement would be how many are getting involved with their peers. Do you see people creating strategies for penetrating their sphere of influence? Do you find people bringing unsaved peers to outreach events or doing outreach events among their peers? Are you witnessing the involvement of people in the process of building and equipping others? If your evaluation reveals that this priority is more a wish than a reality, then it is time to retool your equipping efforts.

NEVER GIVE UP

In June 1955, Winston Churchill was invited to give the commencement address at a British university. When his moment to address these eager graduates arrived, Mr. Churchill rose to the prolonged applause and deep respect of the crowd. With great effort, due to his declining health, he took his position at the podium and stood for a long pregnant moment before this distinguished audience. Then, with penetrating wisdom and dramatic flair, he spoke these words: "Never give up. Never give up. Never give up!" With that he returned to his seat. Caught off guard by the brevity of his remarks, the crowd sat temporarily in stunned silence until they erupted spontaneously in a thunderous standing ovation.

Restoring the heart of the great commission back to the heart of the local church may not be an easy task. But never give up. You may find progress and change hampered by unexpected obstacles, but never give up. You may find that old values fight against new ways, but never give up. The church has been entrusted with the responsibility of helping believers to successfully carry out the ministry of Jesus Christ. Never give up!

On a "Focus on the Family" radio program in fall 1992, James Dobson said, "One of our greatest challenges lies in the fact that the natural progression of any group of people is downhill, not uphill."* The natural path is away from aggressive purpose. Away from risk-taking boldness. Away from willingness to consider change. Away from consistent growth. Away from the greatest "cause" in the history of mankind.

At every turn, choose to face uphill. Take every opportunity to evaluate your effectiveness in light of great commission priorities and patterns. Settle for nothing less than the heart and model of Jesus when it comes to the life of your church.

Never give up!

CHAPTER 4

QUESTIONS FOR REFLECTION

On the Corporate Level:

1. Having just considered churchwide implications of the great commission, write your own version of a purpose statement for your church.

Our church exists in_____
                                            (community)

for the purpose of _____

_____

_____

_____

*Interview of Dr. James Dobson by Rev. Bill Hybels during "Focus on the Family" radio broadcast, December 8, 1992. Used by permission.

2. If you haven't already done so, go back now and complete the chart mentioned on page 56. List every regular program in the life of your church.

> What observations would you make about the emphases, strengths, and weaknesses of your church's programming?

> How hard was it to determine a specific primary purpose for each program?

> Which two or three programs were the hardest to narrow to a single primary purpose?

> Which programs could make a slight shift in primary purpose and yield greater balance for the priorities of winning, building, and equipping? (And obviously, in what direction would you shift their focus?)

3. Shift gears to consider evangelism for a moment. Imagine stepping inside the mind of an unchurched, unsaved, typical, secular person in your community and/or at your job.

> What are their impressions of the church?

> What kinds of experiences and exposure have they had with the church in general and with the churches in your community specifically?

> What do they think about Jesus Christ?

> What do they think about Christianity and about Christians?

4. What might the people of your church begin doing to knock down some of the misconceptions and obstacles people have toward Christ, his church, and toward Christians?

What kinds of things could be done to help your non-Christian peers become interested in the message and hope of the good news in Christ?

FOR FUTHER CONSIDERATION

Equipping people for the ministries of peer care and peer evangelism cannot begin happening if we don't know where we are going. Together with a small group, spend some time wrestling with answering the following statements. Your answers will give you substance to help you shape programs designed for equipping.

A person who has been equipped for ministry to their peers, including both areas of peer evangelism and peer care, needs both skills and knowledge in . . .

They need to be equipped with the following information/knowledge . . .

They need to be equipped with the following skills . . .

Worldwide Implications

As the last slide fades away into blackness and the final challenge to "go into all the world" is given, another missions conference comes to a close. Flags are boxed up, casserole dishes returned from the potluck, display tables disassembled, and the church returns to normal life. Hopefully people are a bit more aware of the spiritual needs worldwide. Hopefully there is a greater understanding of the strategic work missionaries are doing. Hopefully an enlarged blanket of prayer will cover the cross-cultural work of Christ. Hopefully there will be a greater willingness to get involved financially. And hopefully someone might consider answering the call of God to go out into the harvest field of missions.

Sound familiar?

Sure it does. Most of our churches regularly hold some type of missions conference. The missions conference has become a frequently used tool, with admirable goals and often creative programs. Yet we usually treat missions as something wholly different from local ministry.

We act as if local church ministry operates on one set of priorities and missions operates on another. With great fanfare we praise missionaries as people who have given up everything to fulfill the great commission. Yet missions is not a separate enterprise, operating under an agenda different from that of the local church. The great commission was not given as the exclusive property of missions while normal believers and local churches live by a different mandate.

Now, please don't misunderstand. Bringing the gospel into another culture is a complex and demanding process. To underestimate missions would be naive at best. Those who make a commitment of their lives to cross-cultural work are to be held in great esteem.

The goal of this chapter is simply to help us consider some of the implications of the great commission for the national and global work of the kingdom in which we are involved.

TEAR DOWN THE WALLS

We come to the final leg on our journey. To this point we have sought to understand the principles, priorities, and patterns laid out for us in the great commission. We have looked closely at its implications on a personal level and have considered how we might restore its priorities to the heart of the local church. Now we stop to examine the implications of the great commission on the cross-cultural work of Christ and our participation in it.

How do the priorities of the great commission affect our understanding of missions? How do these principles affect our selection of missionary candidates? And what does the great commission tell us about the goal of our missions efforts?

The priorities, principles, and patterns discussed throughout this book are applicable to individual believers and local churches, regardless of cultural or geographical situations. There is one work of Christ and one agenda for the process of making disciples. To that end it is time for us to realize that there are no walls between local churches and missions efforts, only miles. It is time to recognize that we are involved in one work under the leadership of one Savior, regardless of the geographical or cultural setting of our ministry. And it is time to apply the same priorities on a global level that we have discovered for individual believers and the local church. It is time to increase the aggressiveness of our partnership together.

WHOM SHALL WE SEND?

Consider this. Both the priorities of the great commission and the pattern of Jesus' life call us to winning, building, and equipping priorities. His mandate is for each of us to define the task of our life's work as making disciples of our peers. This is the mandate for every believer, the agenda for every church, and the command for every missionary.

While most believers have been sent by Christ into the natural mission field of their own peers, missionaries have the added responsibility of uprooting their lives and becoming a peer to strangers in another culture. God's call on their lives to establish a new peer group among people of a new culture, new land, and new language doesn't alter the fundamental priority of their commission. Once they have established a new sphere of influence in a new land, their task is identical to those that have already been discussed as applying to the rest of us.

Therefore, it only makes sense to send out those who have already demonstrated proficiency at winning the lost, building believers, and equipping workers. We must seek missionary candidates who have established a lifestyle of reaching their peers at home. Each local church and each sending agency should send people who have shown effectiveness at home, where the barriers of culture, language, and geography have been at a minimum. This standard should apply to everyone pursuing vocational ministry.

This was the pattern of the early church. When the leadership of the church sensed God calling them to send some of their own out into ministry to new areas, whom did they send? Paul and Barnabas. They chose two men who were gifted and godly and who had a track record of effectiveness. They sent two of their best people! And the result? Christianity grew like wildfire along the route of their journeys.

It is time for us as the North American church to ask ourselves a tough question or two. Is it possible that because we view the work of cross-cultural ministry as something unique and different from local ministry that we have been lax in demanding that missionary candidates demonstrate effective ministry among their peers at home? Is there a chance that we as churches have been less than discriminating in choosing those whom we will support? How can we afford to send people cross-culturally who have not been effective in their own culture, where barriers are at a minimum? To do so could be a tremendous waste of kingdom resources.

With limited resources and almost limitless global needs, we must send people with demonstrated experience and ability in cross-cultural settings. We may want to consider praying actively about people we should send out rather than waiting for potential candidates to come to us. We ought to be looking around to see if there are Pauls and Barnabases among us, whom God is already using, to call out for full-time ministry. With the world coming to our doorstep, there are growing opportunities to turn people loose into cross-cultural ministry, but wherever they serve, those we appoint must reflect the pattern of Christ found in his everyday commission.

WHAT IS OUR GOAL?

Our goal nationally and globally is consistent with all of our previous discussion about the great commission. It is to establish local ministries that will help God's people win their peers to Christ, build them up in their faith, and equip them to reach their peers. Just as local churches exist to help individual believers fulfill the great commission, so also our national and global efforts ought to help local churches help individual believers.

Imagine for a few moments that a missionary couple is heading to a new location to establish a new ministry. They are going with the clear purpose of establishing a church with indigenous leadership as quickly as possible.

Following the pattern of the great commission, where would they begin? First of all, they will build relationships with people. Learning the language, the customs, and the culture is a part of establishing relationships. These relationships will form the bridge for the gospel, which will soon become a natural part of their conversation.

Communicating the love and truth about Christ may involve physical acts of compassion in response to social and human need, but they will never lose sight of their purpose: to make disciples who can reproduce themselves.

As people respond to Christ, our missionaries will begin working to build them up in their faith—to help them establish roots. Efforts to relate to and win others won't stop, but instead their work will include both areas of winning and building.

After these new believers begin to take root, our missionaries will be faced with the most critical choice of all. Do they keep themselves at the center of the work, or do they pass the ministry on to others? Do they do all the evangelism and nurturing themselves, or do they equip others to do it? Jesus was crystal clear in the great commission.

They now begin to equip young believers to reach their peers and to nurture and build those they win to Christ. The missionaries equip others, who can in turn win, build, and equip others. The ministry at this point has gone full circle. On a personal level, missionaries still win people to Christ and build them up in their faith. But they also equip those who come to Christ to follow the same pattern they are modeling before them.

If you can picture this process, you can picture the explosive nature of the pattern in the great commission. You can also see why those we appoint to full-time ministry need experience and effectiveness in all three priorities of the great commission. Their lifestyle not only initiates the work of the gospel among the lost, but also models the pattern that their followers need to emulate.

What about those who go into support ministries with missions agencies? In some ways they may be different in the full-time focus of their work, but in other ways there should be no difference at all. Just as every Christian in every generation has been given the mandate to follow the great commission, so those who serve in support roles in cross-cultural and international ministries live by the same mandate. In whatever community, culture, or nation they reside, they are called to make disciples as a way of life in the same way all of us are. They have the chance to model the Christian life as well as impact a new sphere of influence. They have the chance to reach people through redemptive relationships just as everyone else does, whether they serve as printers, computer specialists, mechanics, pilots, or in any other capacity.

THE EXPLOSIVE PARADIGM

Many speakers and writers have discussed the geometric growth potential of people who begin working to reach others. If one person reaches one person for Christ in a year and trains that person to do the same during the next year, and if that simple process continues annually, then it would only take thirty-two years to reach the entire planet. It is an exciting concept, but here is an even better one.

What would happen if churches, missions organizations, and denominations all around the world began following the great commission as we have discussed it? If we all began working together to help one another win our peers to Christ, build them up in the faith, and equip them to reach their own peers, the explosion would be incredible.

We would stand back and watch an entirely new sweep of the Spirit of God across the land. And we would sense the presence and power of God as never before. Those who commit themselves to the priorities of the great commission as individuals, as local churches, and as organizations within the body of Christ can claim the special presence and power of Christ in their midst. The reason for this is simple. We have linked arms with the Savior in the central passion of his life!

If around the world we would share this purpose, if we would commit ourselves to aggressive pursuit of the great commission, then we would witness explosive growth and the powerful presence of Christ. We would see the fulfillment of those deep desires expressed by Ron and Alan and the people of their church in chapter 1. We would reclaim our position as the light of the world and the salt of the earth. And the gates of hell would tremble.

CHAPTER 5

QUESTIONS FOR REFLECTION

1. Complete the following sentences:

   Missionaries are . . .

   Missionaries are called to . . .

   Missionaries are just like other believers because . . .

   Missionaries are different from other believers because . . .

2. What standards, abilities, experiences, and gifts have we traditionally looked for in the missionaries we would support? Are there any differences in those standards when examining a potential pastoral candidate? Do you see any changes or additions that should be made in those criteria?

3. You have been appointed to chair a committee that is planning an upcoming missions conference. You have been challenged to help people become enthused about living as missionaries to their own community in their own generation—living by the same priorities of the great commission in their everyday lives as those who are devoted to full-time cross-cultural ministry. What could be said or done as part of this "conference" to accomplish that goal? (This is a tough question, but it is exactly the kind of challenge facing us in our churches. Take your time, have some fun, and perhaps reconvene that small group for discussion.)

4. What are some of the needs we have that compelled Jesus to include the special promise of his presence and authority as part of the great commission?

5. Can you think of anyone in your fellowship who might benefit right now from the encouragement of that promise in Matthew 28:18-20? What could you do to express that encouragement to them? When will you do it?

IT'S THE NEWEST THING IN DOOR TO DOOR EVANGELISM... YOU PUT YOUR TESTIMONY ON TAPE, RING THE DOORBELL, TOSS THE TAPE... AND RUN!

A Personal Journey

We began this book with a very real story about fictitious people. Real, because the story was about intense questions and honest struggles that every genuine believer considers from time to time. Fictitious, because the story was not about specific people nor a particular church, but about characters that represent all of us. We end the book with a true story about real people on a real journey to become great commission disciples.

This journey has been neither painless nor brief. It is not the tale of mystical experiences around inspirational campfires nor of earthshaking conversion records. It is about one couple who began to evaluate the patterns and priorities of their lives and saw the need for change. It is a story of real people who are desperate to make a real difference, but struggle with the plague of ordinariness. This story is about me, Gary, my wife, Margaret, and the ways God has been reshaping our lives. It is far from over.

Earlier in the book we told the story of Dann and his strategy to reach his neighbors. Watching that process in Dann's neighborhood is loads of fun, like a spiritual adventure unfolding before your eyes. But now it is our turn to be a little vulnerable. It's time to pull back the curtains of our lives and look at our journey, in the hope that others with backgrounds like ours might discover new dimensions in living out the great commission.

THE DAY THE LIGHT WENT ON

I remember the discussion as if it were yesterday. We were reminiscing over old times and people who were students in our youth group during earlier days when I had served as a youth pastor. It was a pleasant discussion filled with warm fuzzies, frequent laughter, a few tears, and plenty of questions about who was doing what where. We thought about events, decisions, graduations, engagements, weddings—some moments we'll never forget and even a few we wish we didn't remember.

Somewhere along the way I told Margaret of the growing conviction the Holy Spirit was nurturing within me. I had come to recognize that in spite of all our discussions about evangelism and all our efforts to help students reach their peers, we as a couple had not been regularly involved in reaching our own peers. We believed in the need for Christians to reach out to their unbelieving peers, but there was a definite gap between our beliefs and our actions. We didn't even have *any* significant relationships with non-Christian peers during those years. The truth hit hard.

In spite of what I believed in my head and taught in my ministry, I had lived by a different pattern. My lifestyle proclaimed that building relationships with non-Christians and attempting to reach them for Christ can be an option and need not be the norm. I was working to help students reach their peers, but had no peers of my own who did not know Christ.

But God hasn't called me to a ministry of evangelism among adults right now, I told myself. *My calling is to win students to Christ, build them up in their faith, and help them reach other students.* I didn't have time. After all, I was swamped with junior-high and high-school students, their parents, youth staff, board meetings, Bible studies, and church fellowship activities, not to mention my young family.

Unwittingly, I bought into the notion that evangelism is crucial for the body of Christ in general, but optional in my life. I felt my own giftedness and my vocation added a special justification for this optional plan. I saw the need for reaching my own peers as an extra burden for my full life rather than a source of deep joy. My life was already overly stuffed and had no room for another "burden" of any kind. As a result, however, I missed the fullness of God's plan.

I now realize that in the very process of giving 100 percent of my energy to serve those students and families I deeply loved, I actually shortchanged them. I modeled a deficient portrait of the normal Christian life.

It hurts to recognize that failure.

My heart aches to realize, let alone admit, that Margaret and I had duplicated the common pattern of so many adult believers who have little or no involvement with non-Christians. We had shown those students we loved a lifestyle that was less than what we knew God desired for them.

My excuse was my ministry. After all, I was already serving Jesus. But excuses are hollow, and in the past tense they sound a bit silly.

As Margaret and I talked that day, we started a conversation that has continued on and off since then. We have had to sort out some of what we have been taught about the Christian life, about ministry, and about evangelism. We have begun to shift our priorities. And we have begun to taste the joy that comes when working to reach your peers is no longer just another burden.

BACK IN THE BEGINNING

We need to back up and share a little background about the two of us—not because we desire to criticize those who taught and shaped us, but because our journey has required us to examine the experiences and influences that forged and defined our values. Those forces that shaped our lives are not unique. They have possibly influenced you as they did us.

Margaret and I were raised in Christian families and have been attending church since we were a gleam in our fathers' eyes and a discomfort to our mothers' bladders. If we'd known how to speak, we might have sung "Just As I Am," in the delivery room. We both gave our lives to Christ at a young age, faithfully attended church, won awards in Sunday school, memorized Scripture in Vacation Bible School, experienced the excitement of summer camps, participated in youth group activities, and grew up secure in our salvation. We are blessed recipients of a great heritage of faith, one we are pleased to pass on to our own children. However, along the way, we acquired at least four stumbling blocks, which limited our involvement in reaching our peers. Odds are, you have run into some of these roadblocks, too.

Socially, we learned to build our lives around activities at the church and around relationships with other Christians from church. This pattern, established at an early age, was deeply ingrained by the time we were adults. It seemed natural, even wise, for a Christian to build his or her life entirely around the encouraging fellowship of believers, separate from the negative influence of the world. So that's what we did. Only problem was, when it came to evangelism, we had no relationships with non-Christians with whom we might naturally share the gospel.

A second stumbling block came when we picked up the understanding that the normal Christian life is merely a matter of growing in our relationship with Jesus Christ. We viewed the Christian life in terms of "Jesus and me and what I get out of a relationship with him." It meant attending Bible studies, participating in church events, meeting needs of other believers, and more. With this perspective on the normal Christian life, evangelism became an extra burden above and beyond the normal call of duty. Of course, evangelism was important and something everyone should consider doing, but it was not a central thing. It was in a category all its own, important and desirable, but extra. And since our lives were already consumed by activities and relationships with other believers, there just wasn't any time or energy left for "extra" stuff—especially such alien stuff as regular involvement in reaching nonbelievers.

We also found that we stumbled over our understanding of the evangelistic process. We grew up learning two models of evangelism. The first came in the form of altar calls at the end of a structured service or evangelistic rally. The second model came in the evangelistic training we received. We had been taught the "package approach" of presenting the gospel and then inviting someone to make a decision. Don't get me wrong! There is nothing wrong with either of these two models. They both have an important place. However, neither of these two models fit into the day-in-and-day-out interaction of an ongoing relationship. There are definitely times to invite your friends to make a decision, but altar calls and gospel ultimatums don't fit into normal conversations.

In an ongoing relationship, it is natural to talk about the issues of life over the course of routine activity. If anything is important to you, then it's fair game for discussion. Therefore, in a normal relationship, it wouldn't be right to ignore the subject of Jesus until "the right time" and then bury your friend by unloading the whole gospel dump truck. You share bits and pieces with them and walk with them at *their* speed as the Holy Spirit draws them to Christ. Margaret and I had to recognize that we had held back from evangelism because we had never learned how to win our peers as a normal part of life.

A fourth stumbling block was found in the perception that winning someone to Christ was something you have to do all on your own. We had been led to believe that evangelism was a lone-ranger activity. After all, it was always referred to as "personal evangelism." Team efforts were limited to planned excursions into "foreign territory," where we would witness to people we did not know and would probably never see again. We had no easy way to involve other Christians in an effort to reach our peers, and we had no way to team up with anyone else to help them reach their peers. Helping people overcome their barriers to faith takes time, plus positive exposure to Christians, the church, and Christ, but we had been taught to believe we should do it all alone.

So we were stuck. No wonder it was such a hurdle. According to the models we'd learned, we would have to squeeze in extra activity to be with people we didn't know in order to find the right time to drop the gospel bomb, and be prepared to pick up all the pieces single-handedly. All the while we knew that any mistakes could jeopardize someone's eternal destiny. Makes me tired and anxious just remembering those dynamics.

Conclusion? There had to be a better way. We would have to learn how to work with each other and with other believers to reach our peers for Christ.

THE LEARNING CURVE

Neither of us are gifted evangelists. We have been brought into what we suspect will be a lifelong learning curve. We have discovered the joy of looking at employment in a new light, watching God open new doors for relationships with non-Christians, learning to team up with others, and even looking at the ministry of the great commission apart from ministry titles. Facing our needs and admitting our failures in the past has been painful, but it has created a brokenness that makes every step of progress with someone toward Christ all the more exciting.

We've learned that the normal Christian life includes the joy of involvement in reaching non-Christians, not because it is a job title, not to gain illustrations for sermons, but because that is what we are supposed to do. Developing new relationships and walking with people toward the Savior is the greatest adventure of life. Here are a few examples.

A few years ago, as our children grew older, it became necessary for Margaret to return to work. Initially we saw her work as a means of meeting family needs. No big deal; God provided a job, and that was what we had prayed for. However, we have come to realize that her work is a major door into the lives of non-Christians. Any job has its rewards as well as its drawbacks, but when it becomes the vehicle for eternal opportunities, the whole job takes on a new perspective. Her work became a missions outpost, a place to watch for people apart from Christ with whom we might build a friendship.

As God gives Margaret a natural affinity with someone she works with, she just takes the next easy steps. She'll go to lunch with them, invite them over for dinner, and when there is an appropriate opportunity, invite them to an event at church. In the normal course of conversation she gets a chance to talk about our church, and that always opens doors to talk about where they are spiritually. I've been able to team up with her when there have been male coworkers who share interests of mine. For instance, since I like to play golf, that has become a natural bridge to other men who share my interest. And because our church holds an annual men's golf tournament as an outreach, it has been easy for me to invite some of her coworkers to join me.

Ministry is no longer the same for me, either. I serve as the pastor of a church, but I have come to understand that the work of the great commission is not the same thing as my job. Being a pastor is not what enables me to participate in the work of Jesus Christ. Being a believer gives me all the credentials and all the mandate I need. My obligation is not to be a pastor first, but to follow Jesus: to grow as a disciple of Christ and to make disciples of others. When people see my life, they need to see an example of the normal balance and beauty of the great commission, not a job description. Winning, building, and equipping people for Christ is my privilege, as it is for every believer. As a result, I have more fun and experience more freedom as a pastor than ever before. Being a pastor who is able to serve his flock full-time is an added blessing.

Just like everyone else, I meet other people who are parents of my children's friends, I run into old buddies from the past, I meet people in the community or in my neighborhood, and I become acquainted with friends of people in my church. I will never hit it off with everyone, but there are those with whom I will feel a mutual affinity. When that happens it is natural to consider getting together socially and seeing if a relationship can be formed. As long as I keep my eyes open, I get to watch God move people into my sphere of influence. Those with whom a friendship forms are those whom God is moving into my sphere of influence.

One of those people who has become a very close friend is a man "still in escrow." We do all kinds of things together and share a friendship that is meaningful for both of us. We talk about our kids, about our work, about events of normal life, and about the Lord. God has used the other men in our church body to help rebuild some of his attitudes about Christians and about Christ. And slowly a lifetime of questions and defenses are being resolved. Step by step he is moving toward Christ, and I am getting the incredible privilege of watching the miracle happen before my eyes.

I left out the names and details about these relationships because these people aren't projects. They are our friends. We pray for them and desperately want them to come to know Christ, but we also love them as friends and enjoy their company. Knowing that it can take relationships with several Christians before a non-Christian may trust the credibility of our message, we don't feel compelled to unload the gospel dump truck on them. We cherish the chance to talk about Christ, his church, and the reality of our faith in the course of normal conversation. Because it happens so naturally and we are free to involve others on the "redemptive team," our fears of great extra burdens have never materialized. The only real burden we feel is our desire for the salvation of our friends, and that burden can only be carried in prayer.

A SECOND CHANCE AT THE PAST

That's the journey on which God has been taking us. Yet it might be helpful to take one more look back at our years in youth ministry. It is easy to take potshots at the past from the safety of the present, but if I had a second chance at those years, could I have changed things? Having heard my criticism of the pattern of our life, you deserve to hear how I would apply the lessons I have learned to the real world of those years and see what changes could have been made. Here's a brief list in the hope that these thoughts shed one final bit of light onto your desire to live a great commission lifestyle.

The greatest hurdle keeping us from active involvement in reaching our peers was that we lived by a value system that focused our lives almost exclusively around other believers.

Although this sounds like a nebulous area to change, it really is the first place to start. As long as we believed evangelism to be an extra burden and not a normal joy, we filled our lives with other things first. When building relationships with non-Christian peers is as normal and important as other "normal and important" activities, it cannot help but shape the way you spend your time. Therefore, the first change would be a change of values—a change of outlook.

Second, we would begin looking for people with whom we might initiate relationships.

Since we had no significant relationships with people outside the church, we would have to look for people with whom we could form them. In retrospect, it is amazing how many arenas we were involved in where we could have begun such relationships. There were other parents from the kids' school or from our son's soccer teams, neighbors, parents and family members of the students in our ministry, and friends of our friends at church. These contacts already existed and would have required little or no extra effort. We just weren't looking.

Third, we would shift the settings in which we participated in our favorite activities.

Take softball for example. I enjoyed playing on the church team in the city church league; why not join a team in a nonchurch league? Why not participate in hobbies and athletic or social endeavors alongside people who don't know Christ—and double the benefit? It all boils down to making strategic choices about where we spend our time and looking for people with whom we might build relationships.

A fourth step we would take is the simple step of saying "no" from time to time.

There were occasions when I could have said no to a church fellowship activity in order to have time in my life for people outside the church. Sometimes the greatest enemy to peer evangelism is our overly committed schedule at church. If we could go back, Margaret and I would have politely declined to be involved in some church activities in order to make time for non-Christian peers and still see our family.

Finally, I would have initiated adult-level outreach efforts.

I would have taken some activities already in place and used my influence to shift the focus from fellowship to outreach. I would have found people to join me in trying to reach my nonbelieving peers, and I would have worked to team up with them to reach their peers. I can look back and see that there were unlimited ways we could have teamed up together, whether in structured large-scale activities or small informal efforts. I wouldn't need to wait for the church to officially plan a special outreach program. It only takes people working together to reach their peers, and I could easily have found others to help me.

WHO SAID IT SHOULD BE DIFFICULT?

Does it all sound too simple? It is simple. Living by the priorities of the great commission is not hard. It is not complicated but straightforward. Not burdensome but joyous. Not for super-Christians, but for every believer. The more Margaret and I understand how simple the everyday mandate of Christ is, the more excited we get.

And in all this simplicity there is great passion. More and more in my job I see the desperation in the world. People who appear to have their lives all together are plagued by deep needs and sorrows, with no place to turn for answers. The world is increasingly a dark and frightening place, without light and without hope. But we have the mystery of the gospel, the hope of mankind, and we have been placed here as the light of the world. It is time for passion to reclaim this land. It is time to bring the great commission back to the heart and everyday life of the local church. And it is time to bring the great commission back to the heart of our own lives on a daily basis.

There will never be a time in your life when God stops calling you to reach out to non-Christians. It is his design for the normal Christian life. It is a key to experiencing the full joy of the Christian life. And wrapped around the text of this everyday commission is the mind-boggling promise of Christ:

> *All authority in heaven and on earth has been given to me . . .*
> *And surely I am with you always, to the very end of the age.*

Perhaps the words are too familiar to catch our full attention. But take a look; the mandate of the everyday commission is sandwiched between the beginning and end of this promise. It is as if to say that those who commit their lives, their families, their careers, their hobbies, their time, their churches . . . those who commit themselves wholeheartedly to the priorities of the everyday commission can claim the authority and presence of Christ in a special way. Make his priorities yours and discover the joy of his promise:

Surely I am with you always.

CHAPTER 6

QUESTIONS FOR REFLECTION

It is easy to be motivated and passionate about corporate matters, things that relate to institutions and to other people, without taking the final steps of personal application. It's time to get very personal. If you need to respond to these questions on a separate piece of paper so that you feel more free to be honest, go right ahead. But take time to reflect and respond to these questions.

1. Describe the pattern and schedule of your life. Now add names of people with whom you routinely spend time, hobbies, recreational patterns, and special affiliations or involvements.

2. If you are like most of us, the first look at our schedules appears to be overwhelming and unbendable; however, sometimes changes are in order. What changes need to be made to your schedule? Are there activities that could be refocused and channeled to new purpose and new priority?

3. If you could start over from scratch, throw out some commitments, eliminate some patterns, and start this season

of your life over, what would you do? How would great commission priorities fit into that new plan?

4. How would you honestly rate the quality of your relationships with unbelievers? Which of the unbelieving peers in your life would you consider good friends? Are there untapped opportunities for potential relationships with unsaved peers?

5. When you think about trying to live out the pattern of the great commission more significantly, what scares you? How does Jesus' promise of his presence and power meet your fears and concerns?

6. Who are the other believers you know with whom you might team up in order to support each other as you integrate these principles? If we had English equivalents to the terms *compadres* or *comrades*, that is what these people could be for you. When could you talk to these people? In what ways could you begin encouraging each other and holding each other accountable for this journey of growth?

About Sonlife Ministries

For almost fifteen years, Sonlife Ministries has trained church leadership. The material in this book has been drawn in part from the Sonlife Strategy Seminar and the Growing a Healthy Church Seminar. Although Sonlife began with a primary focus on youth ministries, our efforts and commitment now are actively oriented toward the entire local church. Sonlife Ministries is deeply committed to developing mature disciples of Jesus Christ. Working as the youth training arm of twenty-three denominations, Sonlife equips youth leaders and volunteer staff with the principles of discipleship as Jesus taught them. We are committed to developing complete, balanced ministries of winning, building, and equipping priorities. We believe the *process* of discipleship will lead to the *product* of individuals uniquely equipped to live the powerful life God's Son provided—the "Sonlife."

Annually twenty thousand leaders experience some aspect of Sonlife training. The ministry has grown out of the Strategy Seminar into a complete series of training seminars designed to equip local church leadership. Training and support tools are now available for ministry staff, volunteers, and student leaders.

Total church track

The *Growing a Healthy Chruch Seminar:* a seven-hour overview of the development of a great commission healthy church. This seminar gives Jesus' foundations for ministry and applies it to the local church.

The *Growing a Healthy Church II* seminar: a ten-hour guided workshop for implementing a winning, building, and equipping balance in your church. Prerequisite: GHC I.

The *Growing a Healthy Church III* seminar: three days of intensive training in being a leader that equips the saints to share in the work of the ministry. Prerequisite: GHC I & II.

The *Growing a Healthy Church IV* seminar: three days of intensive training in being a leader who multiplies leaders.

Student ministry track

The *Strategy Seminar:* an eight-hour overview of the discipling process. The Strategy is the hub of Sonlife's youth training. This seminar draws from the life of Christ and applies his philosophy for reaching this generation for Jesus Christ. Biblically based and principle oriented, the Strategy Seminar is readily transferable to any ministry setting.

Youth Ministry Foundations: eight hours of team training for youth leaders and ministry-level students. Principles from the Strategy Seminar are joined with resources and tools to launch your team into great commission ministry. Workshops cover six priorities for student ministry that provide a biblical foundation for life change.

Advanced I—Dig deeper into the Strategy principles while being equipped with tools for vision, direction, team building, and equipping others to minister. Prerequisite: Sonlife Strategy Seminar.

Advanced II—A seminar designed to teach leadership multiplication skills. Learn the skills of consulting and leadership expansion principles within the movement of a discipling ministry. Prerequisite: Advanced I.

Sonlife Evangelism and Missions Project (SEMP)—Practical evangelism and apologetics training, joined with daily evangelistic experience. This week-long project is designed to prepare students for evangelism in their home church.

Sonlife International

Sonlife training has crossed borders and been implemented in such countries as Australia, Venezuela, Poland, Canada, Germany, and the Czech Republic. Contact the Sonlife office for more information on Sonlife's international vision.

As you seek direction for your ministry, consider Sonlife as a partner in ministry. Sonlife desires each training event to be an encouraging, equipping, and motivating experience for you. The training is biblically based, principle oriented, and team applied. We are excited about your joining the movement of church-centered great commission ministry.

These seminars are conducted annually across North America and overseas. For more information on seminar locations and the training of Sonlife Ministries you can write to:

Sonlife Ministries
1119 Wheaton Oaks Court
Wheaton, IL 60187-3051
(708) 682-2959 or (800) 770-GROW

About the Authors

Dr. Dann Spader is founder and director of Sonlife Ministries. A graduate of Moody Bible Institute, he received his M.R.E. and D. Min. from Trinity Seminary. He has served over twelve years in a pastoral role in churches: ten years as youth pastor and two years as interim pastor in a church-planting situation. Dann and his wife, Char, live in Illinois with their three daughters: Julie, Jamie, and Christy.

Rev. Gary Mayes is a senior pastor at Faith Community Church in Santa Ana, California. He received his B.A. from Biola University and an M.Div. at Trinity Evangelical Divinity School. He is a consultant and trainer for Sonlife Ministries. Gary and his wife, Margaret, have two children.

Dr. Spader and Rev. Mayes have previously coauthored *Growing a Healthy Church* (Moody Press).